REH ★ PRO LESSONS

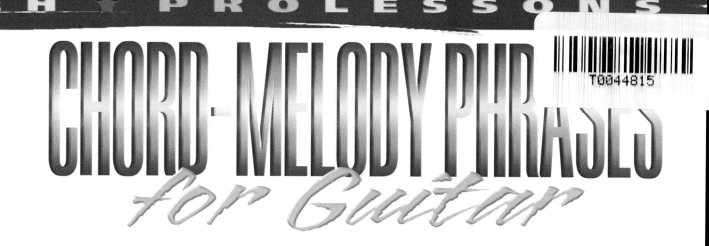

CHORD-MELODY PHRASES for Guitar

by Ron Eschete

PLAYBACK+

Speed • Pitch • Balance • Loop

To access audio visit:
www.halleonard.com/mylibrary

Enter Code
8308-4277-0416-0177

ISBN 978-0-634-02965-3

HAL•LEONARD®

Visit Hal Leonard Online at
www.halleonard.com

Contact us:
Hal Leonard
7777 West Bluemound Road
Milwaukee, WI 53213
Email: info@halleonard.com

In Europe, contact:
Hal Leonard Europe Limited
42 Wigmore Street
Marylebone, London, W1U 2RN
Email: info@halleonardeurope.com

In Australia, contact:
Hal Leonard Australia Pty. Ltd.
4 Lentara Court
Cheltenham, Victoria, 3192 Australia
Email: info@halleonard.com.au

CONTENTS

INTRODUCTION

Since first learning to play the guitar, chords and chord ideas have always fascinated me. The guitar can actually become the entire orchestra—rhythmically, harmonically, and melodically. It can set the entire musical mood: ballads, blues, uptempos, swing, Latin, etc. In this book are some of the licks (phrases) that create such moods as well as different colors and textures. Most of these phrases are part of my repertoire used on a day to day basis and were arrived at by listening to the masters of guitar, piano, horns, and orchestrations, as well as playing gigs with many inspirational players. It is my hope that you will gain a greater understanding of reharmonization by learning and studying the phrases in this book and that you will be inspired to create some of your own.

HOW TO USE THIS BOOK

The chord phrases contained in this book are arrived at through many chord techniques. These may include chord and flat five substitutions, chromatic movements, contrary motion, pedal tones, inner voice movements, and total reharmonization of the harmony. Often throughout the book, you will notice two chord symbols over one chord. In this instance, the larger symbols represent the basic harmony, and the smaller symbols represent the extended or "reharmonized" harmony. I recommend that you compare each reharmonized phrase to the basic chord changes to gain a better understanding of the reharmonization technique. Although most of these phrases were intended for solo guitar, they can usually be incorporated into other contexts; listen carefully to the other instruments in the ensemble and let your ear be the judge. Also be aware that some of the phrases are not necessarily intended to be played along with the basic chord changes.

Phrase #1

Try experimenting with this ii–V–I example either picking each of the melody notes while sustaining the chords, or by hammering-on and pulling-off the melody notes.

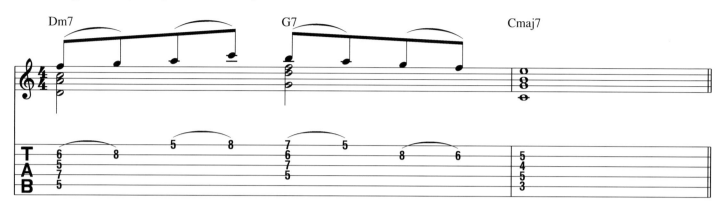

Phrase #2

This simple ii–V–I phrase sounds best if you let the chords sustain for their full value while you play the melody notes on top.

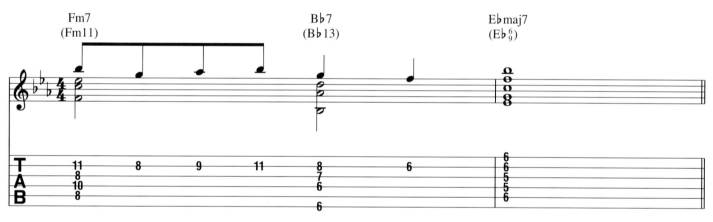

Phrase #3

This phrase is a I–ii–V–I in the key of F. We're using a lot more notes this time. While holding the F and A down, we're playing a melody on top consisting of straight eighth notes.

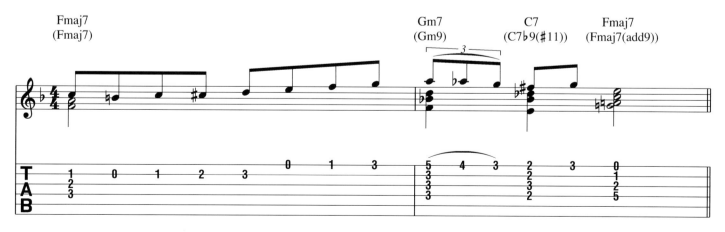

Phrase #4

This phrase demonstrates a iii–VI–ii–V–I in the key of C. I'm using all flat five-type chords: Em7♭5, A7♭5, Dm7♭5 and G7♭5. Also notice the Cmaj9 voicing containing an open E string.

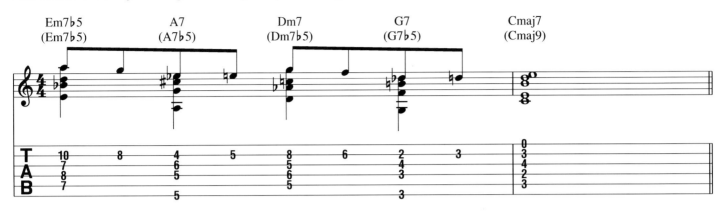

Phrase #5

This chord phrase utilizes a pedal tone (common bass note) under every chord. It's a basic ii–V–I–VI–ii–V–I progression in the key of E♭, while the B♭ pedal maintains a V chord feeling throughout.

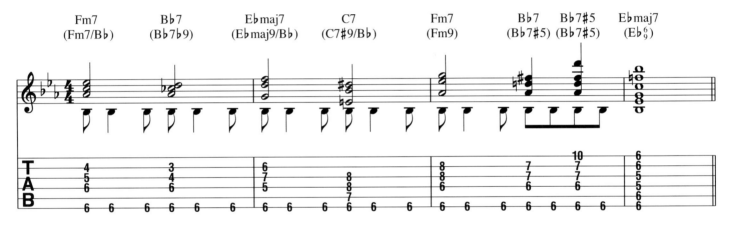

Phrase #6

This example shows a reharmonized I–vi–ii–V turnaround. Although the second, third, and fourth chords (which are all flat five substitutes) can accommodate the melody, they may not sound good when played against the basic changes.

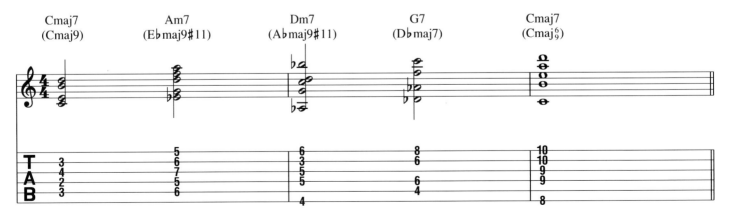

Phrase #7

The second chord in this example is an altered III chord (secondary dominant) in the key of F. This creates a strong resolution to the Dm7 chord. The Ab13 and the Dbmaj9#11 are both flat five substitutes for Dm7 and Gm7, respectively.

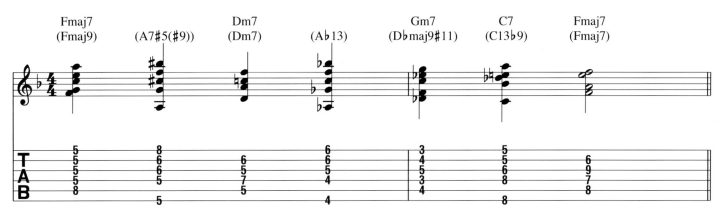

Phrase #8

Here we're using inversions of chords. It's basically a ii–V–I turnaround in F major with a delayed cadence in the V chord (E7#9 instead of C7). Also notice how the closed voicings in the first measure open up for the last two chords. As far as diatonic substitution, in the first measure I'm using a Dm7 for the Gm11, a Bbmaj7 for the Gm9. In the second measure, E7#9 subs for C7.

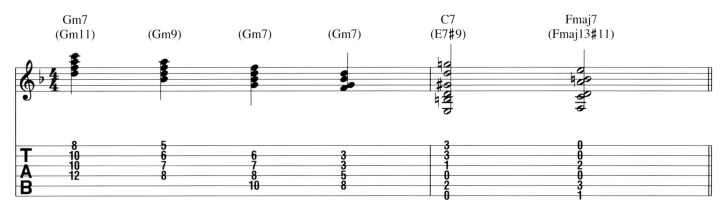

Phrase #9

This phrase uses some nice open-string voicings in the first measure. The last two measures are simply a iiø–V–i into Am.

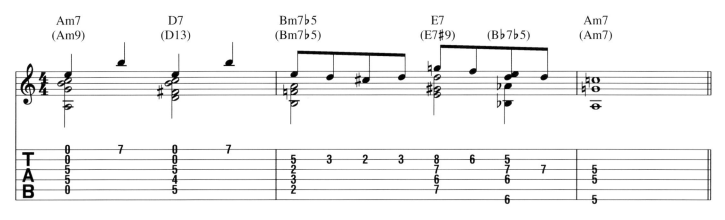

Phrase #10

Here's a ii–V–I in G that works very well as an ending. Although in the first measure we are using thirds to outline the chord, you may want to add the open A string to fill out the sound.

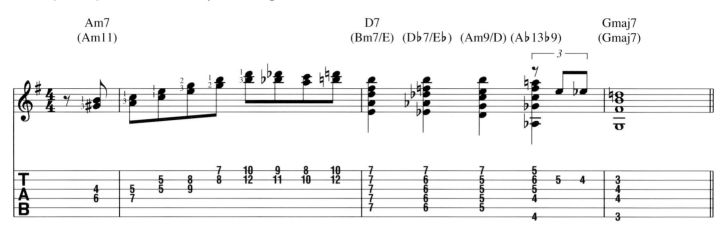

Phrase #11

This basic turnaround phrase uses both closed and open voicings and features flat five substitutes for both dominant 7th chords—D7 and E7. The A13 in the third measure is a secondary dominant (II) chord in the key of G.

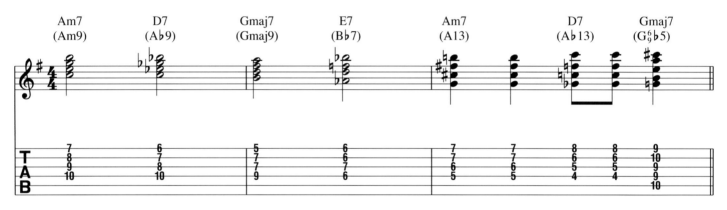

Phrase #12

To play the melody notes in the first chord of this example strum the Cm11, then slide your fourth finger up to the F while keeping pressure down on the string. This gives a nice legato effect. The C♭13 chord is a flat five sub for the F7, and the A13♭9 is a nice passing chord that leads to the A♭13 (a flat five sub for Dm7♭5).

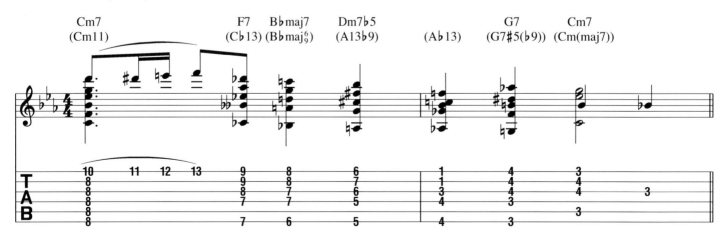

 Phrase #13

This is a blues or static-type lick for A7. Notice how the closed-voiced block chords can sound almost like a saxophone section.

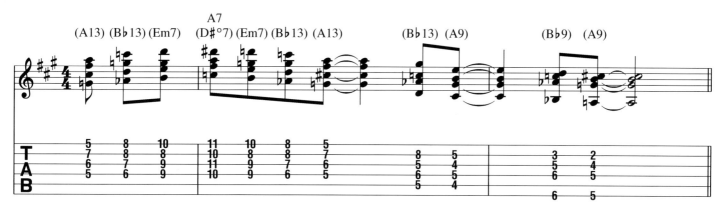

Phrase #14

This phrase is a I–VI–ii passing through the iii chord. It's just a nice isolated lick. You can get away with the G# over the Em chord because it's just passing.

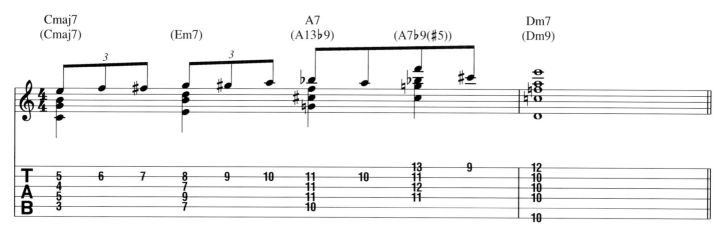

 Phrase #15

Here's a ii–V–I phrase in the key of D. The Bb could be considered the flat five sub of E, but it could also be seen as simply a half-step movement in the V chord (A7). Over the Dmaj7 chord, the melody moves through the dominant 7th (C) down to the 6th (B).

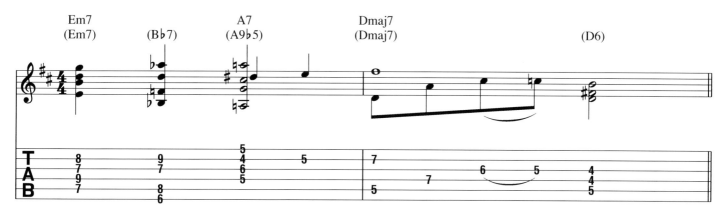

Phrase #16

This is a straight-ahead bop or swing phrase. It begins with diminished passing chords hinting at an E7 sound in the pick up. Notice the nice chromatic movement over D7 targeting the G$^6_9$ chord.

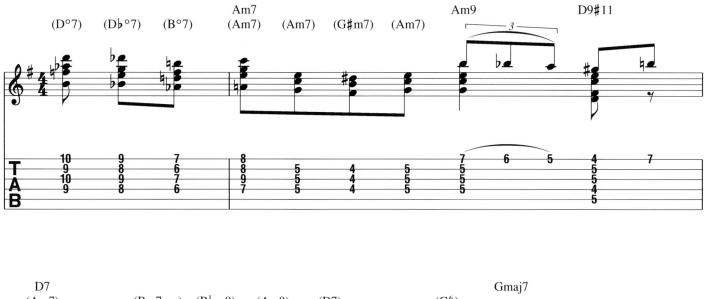

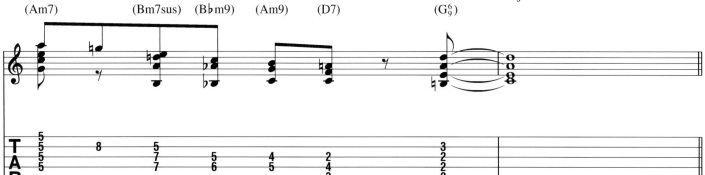

Phrase #17

Here we have another ii–V–I, (Gm–C9–Fmaj$^6_9$). Notice the pianistic line in the first measure moving down to the F chord.

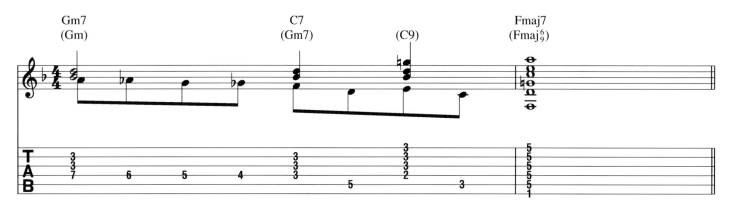

Phrase #18

This could be used as an introduction to an F chord or also as a cadenza at the end of a tune. Notice the slurs on all the different chords. The Fmaj $_9^6$, E♭maj $_9^6$, Fmaj9, E♭maj9, Dm11, and Cm11 are all really functioning as Fmaj7 to E♭maj7 chords.

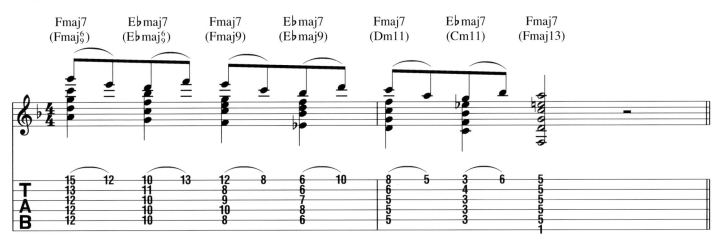

Phrase #19

This example is basically all Cmaj7. We're using passing chords: Cmaj7–Dm7–D♯°7–Em7 (functioning as Cmaj9). It's important to use the fingers on the right hand because the passing sixteenth notes are slurred for the most part.

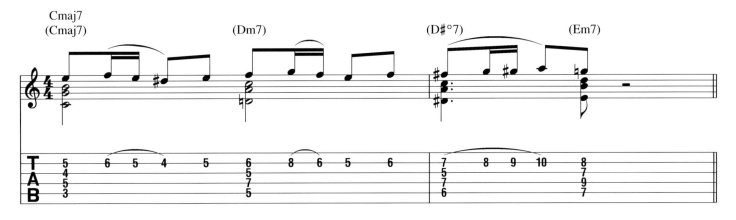

Phrase #20

Here is a ii–V–I progression in the key of C major. The C♯°7 and E°7 chords are suggesting an A7♭9 sound—the V chord of Dm. This technique can create a lot of harmonic motion. The Fmaj7 is simply a diatonic substitute for the Dm7. The F♯m7♭5 serves as a passing chord (which could be analyzed as a D9) and sets up the Dm9/G.

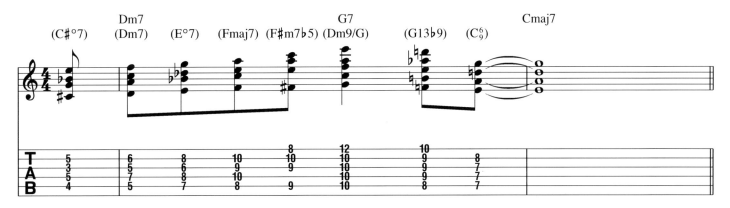

Here is a ballad-style I–vi–ii–V turnaround. We're using flat five substitutes—A♭13 for Dm7, and D♭maj9 for Gm7. The last two measures feature the same progression, but we've added a few passing chords—B♭13 and D9.

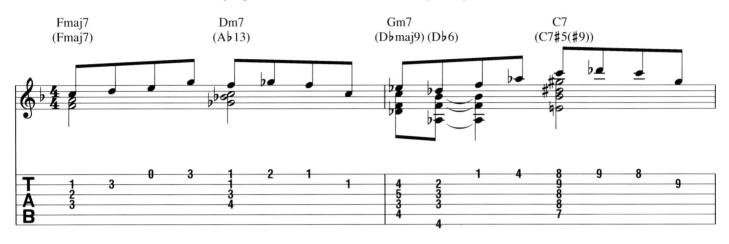

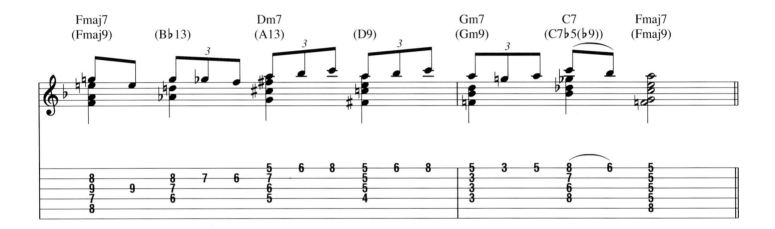

 Phrase #22

The first three chords in this phrase (Dm7–B♭⁶⁄₉–Gm7) basically represent a B♭maj9 tonality. The final chord of the measure (Fm11) leads nicely into a ii–V in the key of Dm. The phrase ends on the iii chord (Dm9) with a major 7th in the voicing for color. So it's just a nice isolated lick, ballad style.

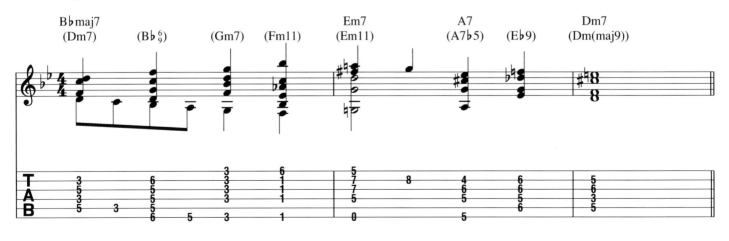

 **Phrase #23**

This phrase could be played in a ballad or swing setting. It's basically a I–VI–ii–V–I progression in the key of E♭. Instead of the usual Fm7 to B♭7, we have an F♯m9 to B9, which moves nicely a half-step into the B♭7.

 **Phrase #24**

This example would be like a tag (ii–V–ii–VI–ii–V–I) on the end of a tune in the key of A♭. Here we utilize the melody on the bottom, which gives us a pianistic effect.

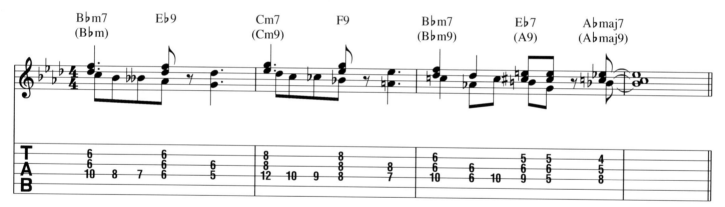

Phrase #25

In this example, we begin with a ii–V–I moving to a dominant IV chord (F13). This leads nicely into the iii–VI–ii–V progression in the third measure. (Note the contrary motion and flat five subs E♭7 and D♭maj7.)

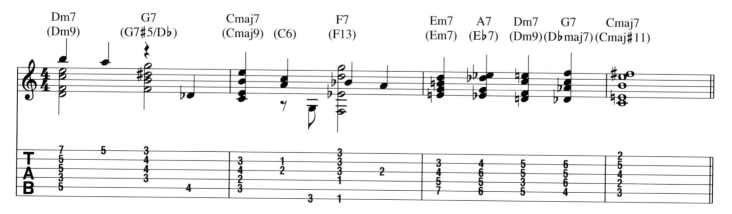

Phrase #26

In this example, we use inversions of chords. Notice how the bass moves up with the melody—G in the bass, C in the bass, E in the bass, etc. The second measure features moving voices on the inside. The next measure uses a flat five sub ii–V, with the V being a major 9 chord (Abm7/Dbmaj9). This would be a good ending or possibly an intro.

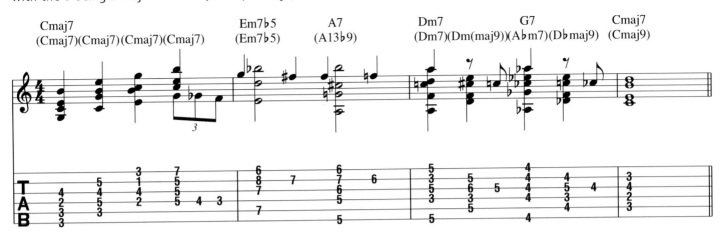

Phrase #27

Here, we have two I–VI–ii–V progressions in the key of C. In the third measure the Cmaj7 moves down to Bb7, setting up the A7. In the next measure, the Dm7sus moves up a half step to Eb9 for melodic purposes, which then moves chromatically down to the Db7#9 (the flat five sub for G7).

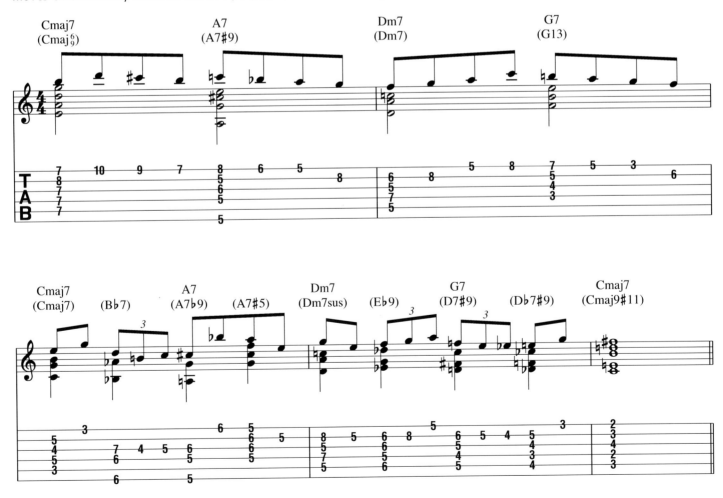

Each measure in this example utilizes contrary motion throughout. Notice the smooth descending bass line:
Bb–A–G–F–E–Eb–D–Db–C–Cb–Bb.

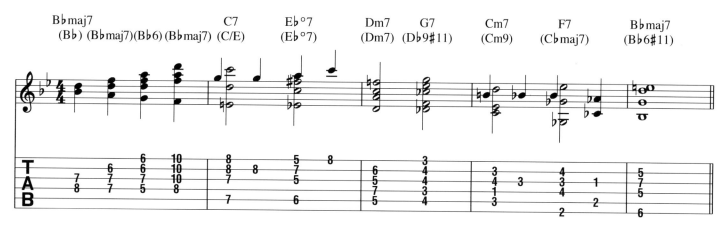

29 **Phrase #29**

Some interesting voicings were used for this iii–vi–ii–V–I progression. For the first chord, we use the open E string and let it ring while we play the Em11 chord. The trick to playing the next two chords (Am11 and Dm11) is to first hit the bass note with the first finger, and then quickly shift up into position for the rest of the chord. Even though the bass notes cannot sustain, the listener still gets the feeling of the full chords.

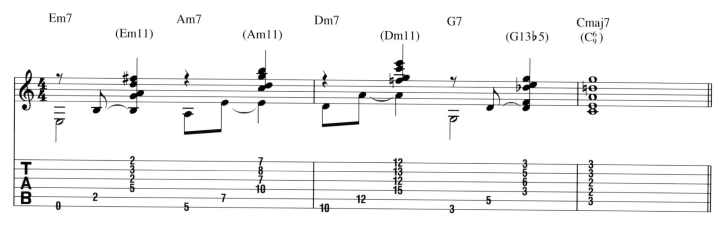

30 **Phrase #30**

This example works best over a static Gm7 or C7 chord. It can be used in a variety of musical styles—jazz, pop, funk, etc. Notice the chromatic movement; certain voicings are simply moved down a half step.

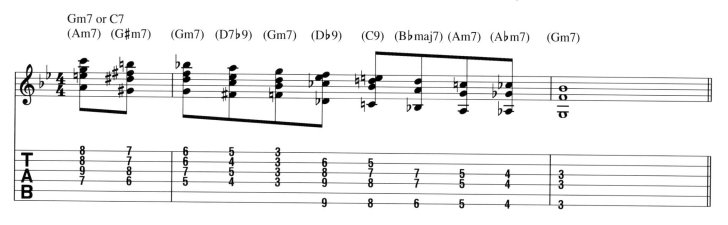

This example fits perfectly over the sixth and seventh measures of a blues progression. The basic changes would be one measure of E♭7 moving back to B♭7. I used a series of diminished chords to reflect the E♭7.

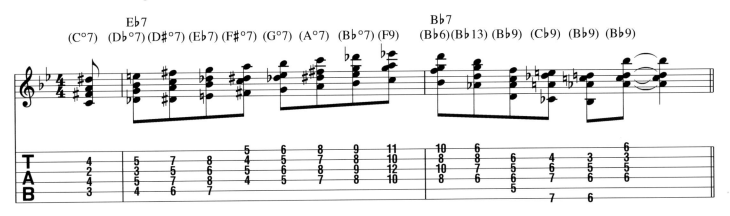

 Phrase #32

This phrase can work very well as an ending. After a I chord, we have a secondary dominant III chord resolving to a vi chord. For the next five chords, I chose voicings that give us a chromatic bass movement from C down to G. In the last half of the fourth measure, notice the use of a flat five substitute ii–V (D♭m9 to G♭7) for C7.

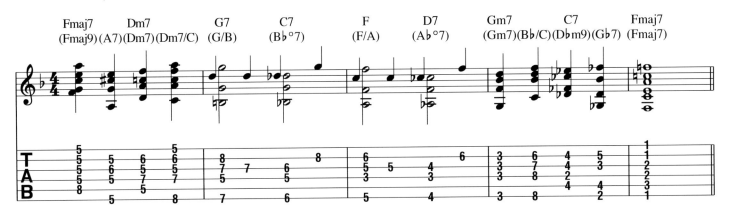

Phrase #33

In this example we're using some contrary motion. The basic changes are Gmaj7 to Gm7, so the first two measures are really Gmaj7 with a lot of chromatic movement.

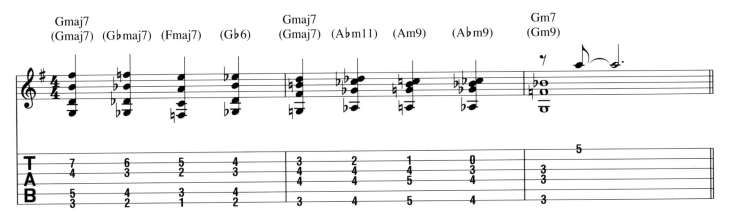

34 Phrase #34

This idea is actually a I–VI–ii–V–I turnaround; it can make either a good intro or ending. The unusual difference here is that we begin with a V chord (F7) sound rather than the I chord. Also notice that the F pedal note (played on every chord except the final one) creates a V chord feeling for all the chords.

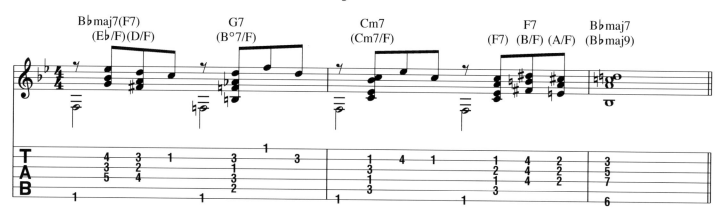

35 Phrase #35

This chord phrase is a I–VI–ii–V–I blues in Eb. In the first measure, I used a little passing progression of Eb7–Fm7–F#°7–Gm7b5 (or Eb9 without the root). Over the second measure (C7), we see Db9, C13, and F#m11. This falls nicely down to the Fm11 in the third measure. For the last chord, I used an Ebm11. This makes for a good ending, as the Ebm11 is very final.

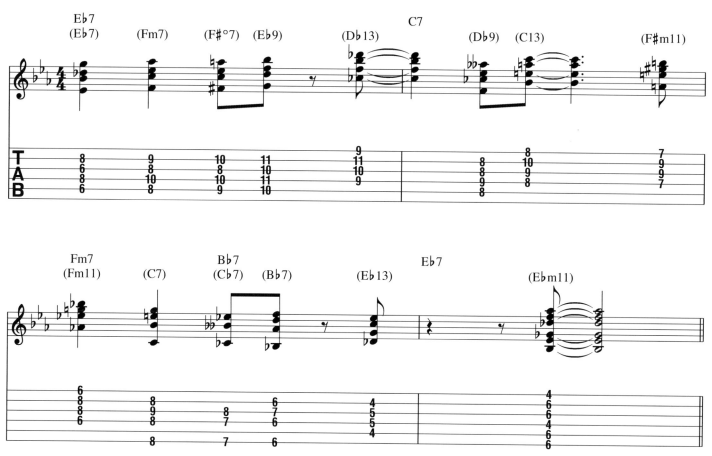

Phrase #36

This short etude is basically in the key of E♭ (or Cm). It is important to sustain the chords while playing the single notes.

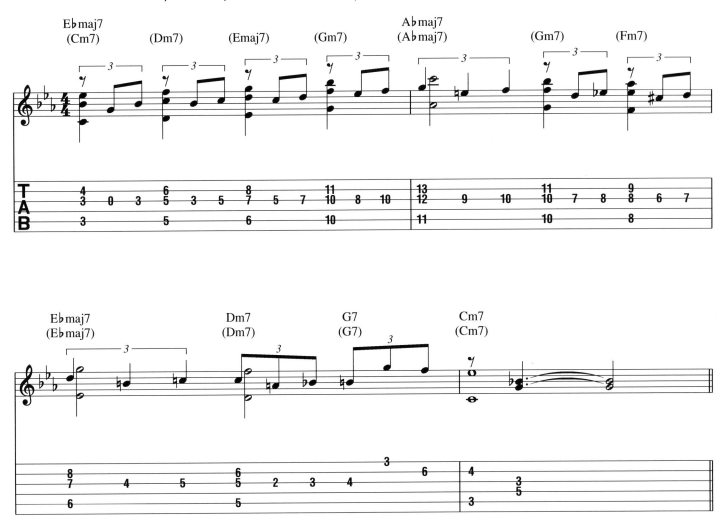

Phrase #37

This chord phrase is in the key of C. It begins with the ii chord (Dm7), but instead of moving to the V (as so often is the case), we move down through a ii°–V–i in A minor. (Notice the descending bass line this creates.) The next phrase (measure 2) is essentially the same material from the first measure, but it has been transposed down a 4th. We finish out with a iii–vi–V progression, making use of a flat five sub (A♭9) over the II chord (D7).

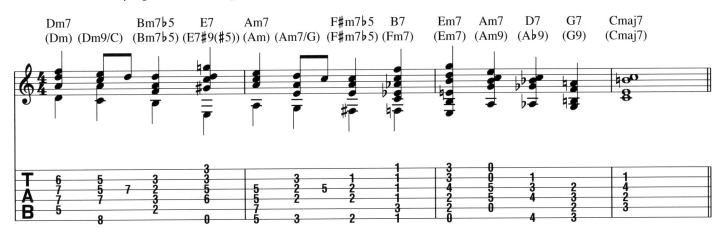

Phrase #38

I play this example with my fingers. It has a walking bass line with a little melody. In the first four measures, a I–vi–ii–V progression is repeated. Notice the passing chords used in these measures—especially the D♭m11 to G♭13 in the third measure. The final two measures start on the flat five (Em7♭5) in the key of B♭ and move chromatically down to an ending. Give it a swing feel.

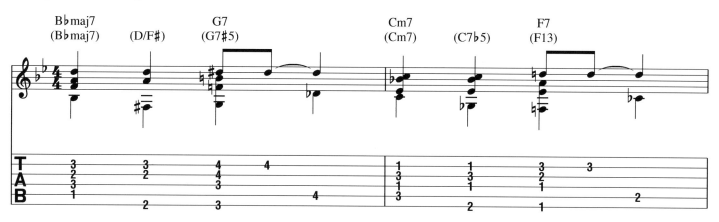

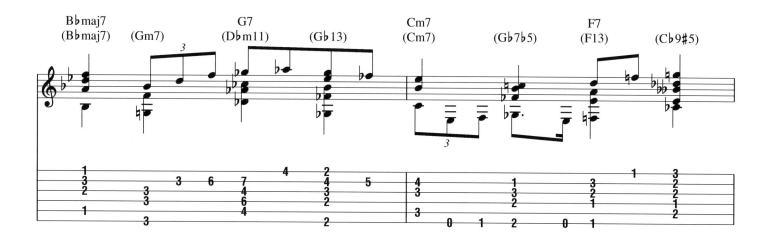

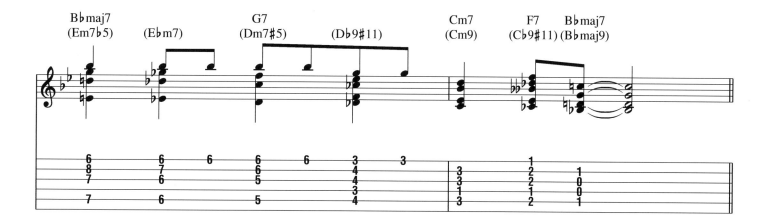

Phrase #39

This final example is a chord solo over a blues in the key of G. You will find some of the various techniques utilized throughout the book. I recommend playing in finger-style. This will help you maintain separation between the melody, harmony, and bass movements.

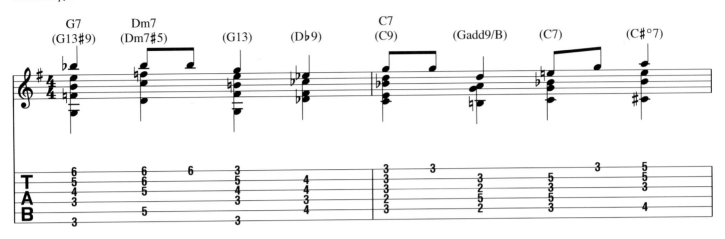

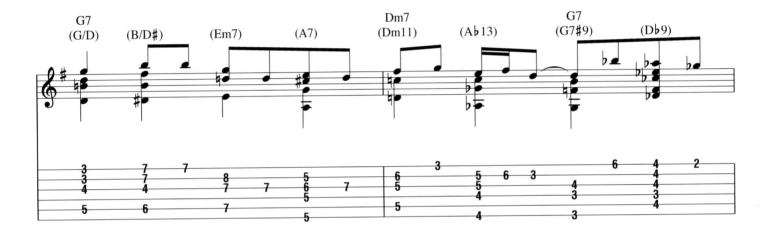

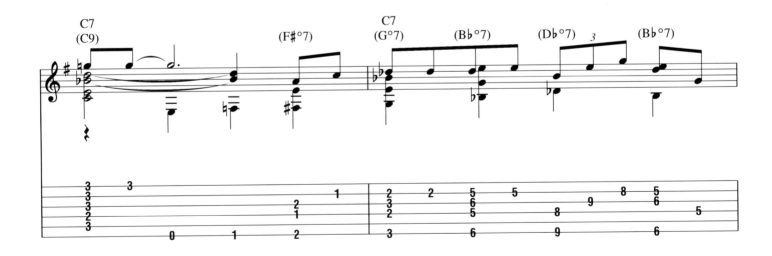

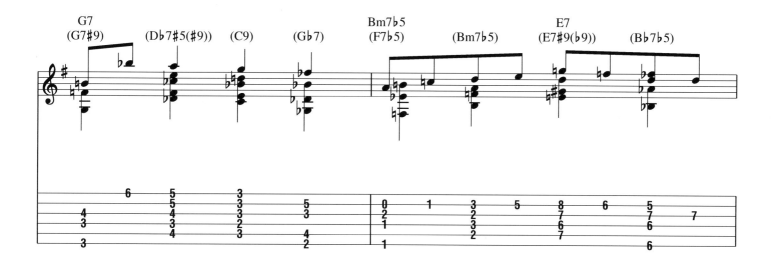

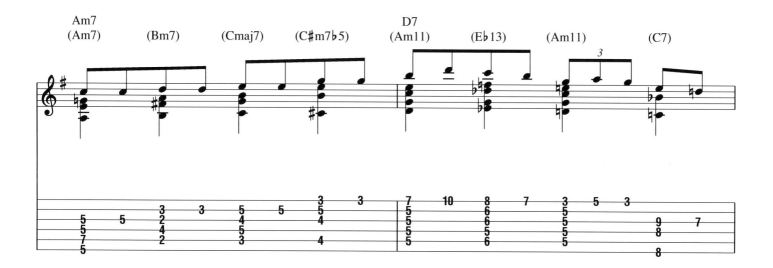

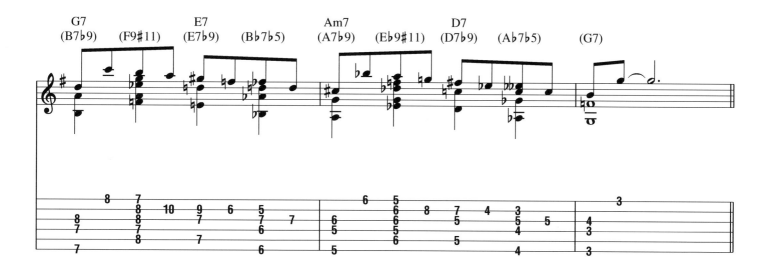

ABOUT THE AUTHOR

Ron Eschete, born August 19, 1948 in Houma, Louisiana, has evolved into a world-class guitarist specializing in chord melody. His incredible sound can be heard on a variety of albums including *To Let You Know I Care* (Muse), *Line Up* (Muse), *Spirit's Samba* (JAS), *"Big Mouth" Milt Jackson* (Pablo), *The Clayton Bros., Johnny and Jeff Clayton* (Concord), *Moon Bird, Time Out of Mind,* and *On a Gentle Note* Dave Pike (Muse).

His television work includes the Merv Griffin show with the Mort Lindsey Orchestra and the Mike Douglas show with Buddy Greco.

Throughout his career, Ron has worked with such greats as Buddy Greco, Milt Jackson, Ray Brown, Hampton Hawes, Warne Marsh, Peter Christlieb, Bob Brookmeyer, and Richie Cole.

While his career has been primarily focused on performance, Ron has dedicated nearly twenty-five years to teaching music at many colleges and universities, including North Texas State University, Utah State University, Loyola University, Louisiana State University at New Orleans, California State Universities at Long Beach and Fullerton, and Musicians Institute in Hollywood.

Ron is currently performing and recording with the Ron Eschete Trio.

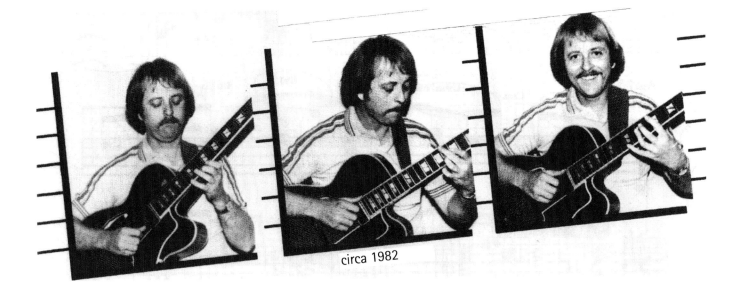

circa 1982

NOTE FROM THE AUTHOR

Of the numerous books that have been written on the subject of chords, I sincerely hope that the various concepts presented here have further provided you with some fresh and stimulating ways to use them. It is important for you to listen to many different musical stylists and build a standard musical repertoire. This, along with your efforts, imagination, and continual experimentation, will help you develop a style of your own.

Ron Eschete

Guitar Notation Legend

Guitar Music can be notated three different ways: on a *musical staff*, in *tablature*, and in *rhythm slashes*.

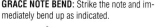

RHYTHM SLASHES are written above the staff. Strum chords in the rhythm indicated. Use the chord diagrams found at the top of the first page of the transcription for the appropriate chord voicings. Round noteheads indicate single notes.

THE MUSICAL STAFF shows pitches and rhythms and is divided by bar lines into measures. Pitches are named after the first seven letters of the alphabet.

TABLATURE graphically represents the guitar fingerboard. Each horizontal line represents a string, and each number represents a fret.

4th string, 2nd fret   1st & 2nd strings open, played together   open D chord

HALF-STEP BEND: Strike the note and bend up 1/2 step.

WHOLE-STEP BEND: Strike the note and bend up one step.

GRACE NOTE BEND: Strike the note and immediately bend up as indicated.

SLIGHT (MICROTONE) BEND: Strike the note and bend up 1/4 step.

BEND AND RELEASE: Strike the note and bend up as indicated, then release back to the original note. Only the first note is struck.

PRE-BEND: Bend the note as indicated, then strike it.

VIBRATO: The string is vibrated by rapidly bending and releasing the note with the fretting hand.

WIDE VIBRATO: The pitch is varied to a greater degree by vibrating with the fretting hand.

HAMMER-ON: Strike the first (lower) note with one finger, then sound the higher note (on the same string) with another finger by fretting it without picking.

PULL-OFF: Place both fingers on the notes to be sounded. Strike the first note and without picking, pull the finger off to sound the second (lower) note.

LEGATO SLIDE: Strike the first note and then slide the same fret-hand finger up or down to the second note. The second note is not struck.

SHIFT SLIDE: Same as legato slide, except the second note is struck.

TRILL: Very rapidly alternate between the notes indicated by continuously hammering on and pulling off.

TAPPING: Hammer ("tap") the fret indicated with the pick-hand index or middle finger and pull off to the note fretted by the fret hand.

NATURAL HARMONIC: Strike the note while the fret-hand lightly touches the string directly over the fret indicated.

PINCH HARMONIC: The note is fretted normally and a harmonic is produced by adding the edge of the thumb or the tip of the index finger of the pick hand to the normal pick attack.

PICK SCRAPE: The edge of the pick is rubbed down (or up) the string, producing a scratchy sound.

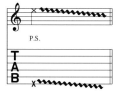

MUFFLED STRINGS: A percussive sound is produced by laying the fret hand across the string(s) without depressing, and striking them with the pick hand.

PALM MUTING: The note is partially muted by the pick hand lightly touching the string(s) just before the bridge.

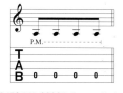

RAKE: Drag the pick across the strings indicated with a single motion.

TREMOLO PICKING: The note is picked as rapidly and continuously as possible.

VIBRATO BAR DIVE AND RETURN: The pitch of the note or chord is dropped a specified number of steps (in rhythm) then returned to the original pitch.

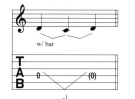

VIBRATO BAR SCOOP: Depress the bar just before striking the note, then quickly release the bar.

VIBRATO BAR DIP: Strike the note and then immediately drop a specified number of steps, then release back to the original pitch.

IMPROVE YOUR IMPROV

AND OTHER JAZZ TECHNIQUES WITH BOOKS FROM HAL LEONARD

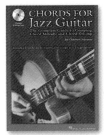

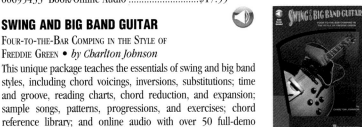